THE COMPLETE MICROWAVE COOKBOOK

THE COMPLETE MICROWAVE COOKBOOK

75 simple recipes ready in minutes

CONTENTS

A GUIDE TO MICROWAVE COOKING

MICROWAVE COOKING

A term like "microwave dinner" conjures up an image of an unhealthy, processed, and low-quality meal, often seen as a last resort for those short of time and energy. Furthermore, the microwave's legacy as a convenient tool for reheating leftovers means their full functional and versatile potential is overlooked and underutilized. While they do indeed save on time, space, energy, and washing up, the microwave's full creative potential goes well beyond this. Using the microwave to create delicious, fresh, and nourishing meals – from start to finish – is not only possible, but often preferable! Additionally, cooking a whole meal in a matter of minutes in the microwave, avoiding long oven pre-heating and cooking times, means it is one of the most energy-efficient ways of cooking.

HOW DO MICROWAVES WORK?

Simply put, using electromagnetic radiation, microwaves excite molecules in food, which, in turn, creates heat. This radiation is exceptionally good at heating water and fat, which luckily are very important requirements of the cooking process! Beyond this basic essential function, the heating of water is ideal for the steaming of vegetables, the boiling of pasta, and the cooking of fish, among many other things. The heating of fat is also incredibly useful for toasting nuts, softening garlic, and making crispy shallots. Be mindful that fat reaches a higher temperature than water, so it is important to check these foods at regular intervals.

TYPES OF MICROWAVE

Microwaves vary in size, look, and, ultimately, price, however they all perform the exact same function of heating molecules – so do not worry if you don't have the most fancy top-of-the-range model, any will do! The majority of microwaves have rotating turntables, which helps to heat food more evenly – if your microwave does not have a turntable, then you will need to rotate the cooking container at regular intervals.

MICROWAVE SAFETY

Safety when cooking on the hob or in the oven should always be a priority, and the same goes for microwave cooking. There are a number of materials that should never find their way into the microwave:

Aluminium foil This will heat up rapidly and risk causing a fire. It is best to avoid putting metal of any kind in the microwave.

Wood This will rapidly dry out and potentially crack. While less of a fire hazard than foil, it can also eventually catch fire.

Recycled kitchen paper Unlike regular kitchen paper, recycled kitchen paper can contain small pieces of metal, which could cause sparking.

Microwave-safe glass and silicone are the only materials that should be used in microwave cooking. Generally, ceramics are also safe, as long as they do not have any metallic element to them, such as an inlay or paint.

COVERING FOOD

When cooking in the microwave it is generally a good idea to cover the food, as it avoids splatters, and it ensures a more even and time-effective cook. However, you should never tightly cover a container as this causes a build-up of pressure. Using a microwave plate or microwave-safe lid with vented holes will allow the steam to escape.

MICROWAVE KIT

The advantage of cooking with a microwave is the small amount of kitchen equipment required. There are just a handful of essentials:

Microwave-safe bowl To keep things nice and simple, the majority of the recipes in this book have been tested in two different sized microwave-safe round glass bowls – a 19cm (7½-inch), 1-litre (4-cup) bowl and a 23cm (9-inch), 3-litre (12-cup) bowl.

Oven gloves A must for safely removing hot containers from the microwave.

Digital thermometer probe To check the internal temperature of certain meats and fish.

WATTAGE AND SETTINGS

All of the recipes in this book have been tested in an 800W microwave. If you have a lower or higher wattage microwave, then please bear in mind that you will have to adjust the timings slightly. Always keep checking the food as you cook.

For these recipes, assume the temperature is always on the highest setting, unless otherwise specified.

DOUBLING RECIPES

If you're doubling up on recipes don't assume doubling the time will achieve the same results – some trial and error is always necessary!

MICROWAVE TECHNIQUES

Here are a few basic cooking techniques you can achieve in your microwave:

Toasting nuts Add 50g (⅓ cup) of nuts to a microwaveable plate, then drizzle over 1 tablespoon of vegetable oil, and mix well so the nuts are coated. Arrange in a single layer on the plate and cook, uncovered, for 3 minutes until they smell toasty.

Making crispy shallots To a small microwaveable bowl, add 2 sliced shallots and 100ml (6½ tablespoons) of vegetable oil. Cover and cook in the microwave on the lowest setting for 8 minutes, stirring at 2-minute intervals, until golden and crispy. Transfer the shallots to some kitchen paper.

Making confit tomatoes Put 200g (7oz) of cherry tomatoes in a small microwaveable bowl and add 1 tablespoon of olive oil. Cover and cook for 7 minutes until the tomatoes have softened.

Making confit garlic Put 1 head of garlic in a small microwaveable bowl, add 100ml (6½ tablespoons) of olive oil. Cover and cook on the lowest setting for 10 minutes until the garlic has softened.

5 BEST FOODS TO COOK IN THE MICROWAVE

1 TENDER, FLAKY FISH

2 GOOEY MUG CAKES

3 THE CRISPIEST BACON

4 PERFECTLY STEAMED VEGETABLES

5 FUDGEY BROWNIES

BREAKFASTS

Rustle up easy breakfasts
without compromising on flavour.
From a hearty breakfast burrito
to fuss-free blueberry muffins,
you'll save on laborious cooking
techniques, which can be tricky
at the best of times, especially
before your first coffee!

BREAKFAST BURRITO

1 avocado, roughly chopped
1 large tomato, roughly chopped
handful of coriander, roughly
   chopped
¼ red onion, finely chopped
juice of 1 lime
4 rashers of streaky bacon
2 eggs
2 large tortilla wraps
200g (1⅓ cups) canned black beans
   (drained weight), rinsed
salt and freshly ground black pepper

TO SERVE (OPTIONAL):
hot sauce

1 To a small bowl, add the avocado, then mash with a fork. Add the tomato, coriander, red onion, and lime juice. Season with salt and freshly ground black pepper, mix well, then set aside.
2 Lay the bacon out flat on a microwaveable plate, cover with kitchen paper and cook in the microwave for 2 minutes. Flip the bacon over, cover with the kitchen paper, then cook for a further 2 minutes. At this stage, if the bacon is not crispy and golden, cook again for 30 seconds.
3 Crack the eggs into a small microwaveable bowl, then whisk well. Cover and cook in the microwave in 30-second intervals for 2 minutes, stirring between each interval, until the egg is set but still a little runny. Set aside.

4 Put the wraps onto a microwaveable plate and cook in the microwave for 30 seconds until warmed through.
5 To assemble, divide the avocado mixture between the wraps, then add the egg, bacon, and black beans. For some heat, splash over some hot sauce, then wrap up and serve.

SWAP IT The fillings are easily adaptable – feel free to swap the bacon for sausages, or, to make this veggie, leave out the bacon altogether. To make this vegan, leave out the bacon and eggs, and replace with Scrambled Tofu (see p27).

Prep + cook time
10 minutes
Serves 2

FULL ENGLISH BREAKFAST TRAY

4 sausages
1 large tomato, halved
100g (1⅓ cups) chestnut
   mushrooms, quartered
1 tbsp extra virgin olive oil
1 tsp dried oregano
415g (15oz) can baked beans
salt and freshly ground black pepper

1 Put the sausages, tomato, and mushrooms into a large microwaveable bowl. Prick the sausage skins with a fork several times. Drizzle the olive oil over the tomato and mushrooms, then sprinkle over the oregano and a little salt.

2 Cover and cook in the microwave for 7 minutes until the mushrooms have softened, are golden in colour, and the sausages are cooked through. Set aside.

3 Put the beans in a small microwaveable bowl, then cover and cook in the microwave for 2 minutes until they are piping hot.

4 Lay everything out on a tray, crack over lots of black pepper, then serve.

SWAP IT To make this vegan, swap the sausages for plant-based ones. Leave out, or add in, whatever you fancy! Bacon or slices of avocado on the side would also work well here.

Prep + cook time
10 minutes
Serves 2

PASSION FRUIT CURD

4 passion fruits
juice of ½ lemon
175g (¾ cup plus 2 tbsp)
    caster sugar
1 egg, whisked
60g (½ stick) unsalted butter

1 Put the passion fruit pulp into a sieve and set over a small microwaveable bowl. Using a spatula, press down on the pulp to extract as much juice as possible. You should have around 40ml (2½ tbsp) of juice. Discard the seeds from the sieve.
2 To the bowl, add the lemon juice, sugar, egg, and butter. Cover and cook in the microwave for 1 minute, then remove and stir. Continue to cook in 30-second intervals, stirring between each interval, for a total of 3 minutes until very thick.

3 Pour into a 250ml (9fl oz) jar and leave to cool.

SWAP IT If you are unable to get hold of passion fruits, instead use the juice of 4 lemons and follow the same cooking process to make lemon curd.

KEEP IT This will keep for up to 5 days in the fridge.

**Prep + cook time
5 minutes
Makes 250ml (1 cup)**

19

SHAKSHUKA

1 red pepper, thinly sliced
½ onion, thinly sliced
1 tbsp extra virgin olive oil
300ml (1¼ cups) passata
2 tsp harissa
2 eggs
100g (3½oz) feta
handful of coriander, roughly
   chopped
salt and freshly ground
   black pepper

TO SERVE:
2 pitta breads

1 Add the pepper, onion, and olive oil to a small microwaveable bowl. Cook in the microwave, uncovered, for 2 minutes until softened.
2 Add the passata and harissa. Season with salt and freshly ground black pepper, then mix well.
3 Make two small wells in the mixture and crack both eggs in. Cover and cook in the microwave for 1 minute, then cook in 30-second intervals for 2 minutes, stirring the sauce between each interval, until the egg whites are set, but the yolks are still runny.
4 Crumble over the feta and sprinkle over the chopped coriander.
5 Serve with pitta breads for dipping.

Prep + cook time
5 minutes
Serves 2

BLUEBERRY JAM

400g (3¼ cups) blueberries
100g (½ cup) caster sugar
1 tbsp lemon juice
1 tsp vanilla extract

1 Put all the ingredients into a large microwaveable bowl. Cover and cook in the microwave for 4 minutes. Stir, then cover and cook for a further 3 minutes until the blueberries have softened and the mixture looks thick and syrupy.
2 Transfer to a 250ml (9fl oz) jar and leave to cool.

SWAP IT Strawberries or blackberries would also work well here.

KEEP IT Store in a glass jar in the fridge for up to 5 days.

**Prep + cook time
7 minutes
Makes 250ml (1 cup)**

PORRIDGE WITH CHERRIES

100g (⅔ cup) frozen cherries
1 tbsp maple syrup, plus
　extra to serve
½ tsp ground ginger
60g (scant ½ cup) rolled
　porridge oats
150ml (⅔ cup) milk
½ tsp ground cinnamon
1 tbsp pumpkin seeds

1 Put the frozen cherries, maple syrup, and ground ginger into a small microwaveable bowl. Cover and cook in the microwave for 2 minutes until the cherries have softened, then set aside.
2 Put the porridge oats, milk, and 150ml (⅔ cup) water into a large microwaveable bowl. Cover and cook in the microwave for 2 minutes, then stir and cook for a further 1 minute until thick.

3 Divide the porridge between two bowls, top with the cherries, drizzle over some extra maple syrup, and sprinkle over the cinnamon and pumpkin seeds.

TIP To keep it even more simple, leave out the cherries, and serve the porridge simply with a drizzle of maple syrup.

**Prep + cook time
7 minutes
Serves 2**

SCRAMBLED TOFU

280g (10oz) firm tofu
½ tsp ground turmeric
½ tsp smoked paprika
2 tbsp milk
handful of fresh oregano,
   leaves picked
salt and freshly ground
   black pepper

TO SERVE (OPTIONAL):
2 slices of sourdough toast
2 tbsp Confit Tomatoes
   (see p11)
1 avocado, thinly sliced

1 Crumble the tofu into a large microwaveable bowl. Add the turmeric, paprika, and milk, then season with salt and lots of freshly ground black pepper. Cover and cook in the microwave for 3 minutes until warmed through. Add the oregano leaves, then mix well.

2 To serve, divide the tofu over slices of toasted sourdough, top with confit tomatoes, and serve with avocado slices on the side.

SWAP IT To make this vegan, swap out the milk for a plant-based alternative.

TIP Add a tablespoon of nutritional yeast, if you have any, at the same time as the milk to make this tofu even creamier.

**Prep + cook time
5 minutes
Serves 2**

BLUEBERRY BREAKFAST MUFFINS

60g (½ stick) unsalted butter, softened
60g (5 tbsp) caster sugar
120ml (½ cup) milk
180g (1⅓ cups) plain flour
1 tsp baking powder
80g (⅔ cup) blueberries

EQUIPMENT

4 x 8cm (3¼-inch) silicone muffin cases, lightly oiled

1 In a medium bowl, cream the butter and sugar together with a wooden spoon until pale.
2 Add the milk and mix until smooth. Add in the flour and baking powder, and fold in using a spatula.
3 Fold in the blueberries, then divide the mixture amongst the oiled muffin cases.
4 Cook the muffins in the microwave, two at a time, uncovered, for 2 minutes until a skewer comes out clean when inserted.

SWAP IT The blueberries can be swapped for either raspberries or blackberries, or even a defrosted frozen berry mix.

Prep + cook time
10 minutes
Makes 4

BANANA MUG CAKE

1 banana, peeled and cut
   into chunks
35g (¼ cup) plain flour
4 tsp maple syrup, plus
   extra to serve
½ tsp baking powder
1 egg
20g (2 tbsp) dark chocolate chips
10g (generous 1 tbsp) almonds or
   walnuts, roughly chopped

1 Add the banana to a small bowl and mash with a fork. Add the flour, maple syrup, baking powder, egg, and chocolate chips. Mix well until combined, then transfer the mixture to a mug.
2 Cook in the microwave, uncovered, for 2 minutes until a skewer comes out clean when inserted.

3 Sprinkle over the nuts, drizzle over a little extra maple syrup, and serve.

**Prep + cook time
4 minutes
Serves 1**

STRAWBERRY COMPOTE

250g (2½ cups) strawberries, hulled, larger ones halved and smaller ones left whole
2 tbsp caster sugar
juice of ½ lemon
1 tsp vanilla extract
1 tsp cornflour

1 Put all the ingredients into a large microwaveable bowl and stir.
2 Cover and cook in the microwave for 3 minutes until the strawberries have softened but are still holding their shape.
3 Leave the compote to cool before serving.

SERVE IT Spoon over plain porridge or yogurt, or spread on toast.

KEEP IT Store in a glass jar in the fridge for up to 5 days.

Prep + cook time
5 minutes
Serves 2

WARMED TOMATOES WITH RICOTTA ON TOAST

200g (7oz) cherry tomatoes, halved
1 tbsp extra virgin olive oil
2 slices of sourdough
1 clove of garlic
60g (¼ cup) ricotta
grated zest of 1 lemon
pinch of chilli flakes
handful of basil, roughly chopped
salt and freshly ground black pepper

1 Put the tomatoes in a small microwaveable bowl and add the olive oil. Cover and cook in the microwave for 7 minutes until the tomatoes have burst and softened.
2 Meanwhile, toast the sourdough, then rub the garlic clove over the toast.
3 Spread the ricotta over both slices of toast, then top with the tomatoes, lemon zest, chilli flakes, and basil. Season with salt and pepper, and serve.

SWAP IT To make this vegan, replace the ricotta with a whipped tofu. Simply blend a block of firm tofu with olive oil, salt, water, and lemon zest until you have a spreadable, creamy consistency.

Prep + cook time
10 minutes
Serves 2

SIDES

Side dishes are often the unsung heroes of a main meal, and with a microwave they needn't be an afterthought. This chapter is full of delicious options for all occasions, from fresh salads to accompany a summer barbecue to zingy vegetable dishes to liven up any Sunday roast.

HASSELBACK POTATOES WITH ZESTY GREEN SAUCE

600g (1lb 5oz) floury potatoes
4 anchovy fillets, finely chopped
handful of flat-leaf parsley,
   finely chopped
2 tbsp fresh oregano, finely chopped
grated zest and juice of 1 lemon
60ml (¼ cup) extra virgin olive oil
freshly ground black pepper

1 Put a potato between two wooden spoon handles and thinly slice through until the knife hits the spoon – this will prevent cutting all the way through the potato. Repeat with the rest of the potatoes.

2 Put the potatoes into a large microwaveable bowl and add 2 tablespoons of water. Cover and cook in the microwave for 10 minutes until tender and cooked through.

3 Meanwhile, in a small bowl, combine the anchovies, parsley, oregano, lemon zest, lemon juice, and olive oil. Mix well.

4 Serve the potatoes with the green sauce spooned over the top.

SWAP IT To make these vegan, simply swap the anchovies in the dressing for a tablespoon of capers.

TIP This recipe can be easily doubled: just make the first batch of potatoes, set them aside under some foil, then repeat with the second batch, and double up on the dressing.

**Prep + cook time
10 minutes
Serves 2**

HOT HONEY CORN ON THE COB

2 corn on the cobs
2 tbsp unsalted butter, softened
1 tbsp hot honey
grated zest of 1 lime

TO SERVE (OPTIONAL):
1 green chilli, thinly sliced
2 tbsp Crispy Shallots
  (see p11)
handful of coriander,
  roughly chopped
a pinch of cayenne pepper

1 To a large microwaveable bowl, add the corn and 2 tablespoons of water. Cover and cook in the microwave for 7 minutes until tender.
2 Meanwhile, to a small bowl, add the butter, honey, and lime zest. Mix well.
3 Put the corn on a plate, dot the butter over the corn, and leave for a minute or two to melt.
4 To serve, top with green chilli, crispy shallots, coriander, and a pinch of cayenne pepper, if you like.

SWAP IT If you are unable to find hot honey, add 1/4 teaspoon of cayenne pepper or chilli powder to 1 tablespoon honey. To make this vegan, swap the butter for plant-based spread, and swap the honey for maple syrup.

Prep + cook time
10 minutes
Serves 2

BROCCOLI WITH LIME & SOY MAYO

200g (7oz) Tenderstem broccoli
2 tbsp mayonnaise
1 tbsp soy sauce
1 tsp maple syrup
juice of ½ lime

TO SERVE (OPTIONAL):
½ red chilli, deseeded and thinly
    sliced
2 tbsp Crispy Shallots (see p11)

1 Put the broccoli into a large microwaveable bowl with 2 tablespoons of water. Cover and cook in the microwave for 4 minutes until tender.
2 Meanwhile, to a small bowl, add the mayo, soy, maple syrup, and lime juice. Mix well.
3 Serve the broccoli topped with sliced chilli and crispy shallots, if you like, with the mayo on the side.

SWAP IT To make this vegan, simply use a vegan mayo.

**Prep + cook time
5 minutes
Serves 2**

POTATO SALAD

4 rashers of streaky bacon
500g (1lb 2oz) new potatoes, halved
½ red onion, thinly sliced
juice of 2 lemons
2 tbsp Greek yogurt
2 tbsp mayonnaise
2 tbsp pesto
1 stick of celery, finely chopped
2 tbsp capers, roughly chopped
2 tbsp cornichons, finely chopped
2 tbsp finely chopped chives
2 tbsp finely chopped dill
salt and freshly ground
    black pepper

1 Lay the bacon out flat on a microwaveable plate, cover with kitchen paper and cook in the microwave for 2 minutes. Flip the bacon over, cover with the kitchen paper again, and cook for a further 2 minutes. At this stage, if the bacon is not crispy and golden, cook again for 30 seconds. Leave to cool, then roughly chop and set aside.

2 Put the potatoes in a large microwaveable bowl and add 2 tablespoons of water. Cover and cook in the microwave for 9 minutes until tender.

3 Meanwhile, in a small bowl combine the red onion, juice of 1 lemon, and a pinch of salt. Scrunch together with your hands, then set aside to pickle lightly.

4 Tip the potatoes into a colander and briefly run under cold water to cool slightly.

5 Transfer the potatoes to a serving bowl, add the juice of the remaining lemon, the Greek yogurt, mayonnaise, pesto, celery, capers, cornichons, chives, dill, and bacon. Season with salt and freshly ground black pepper, then give everything a good mix together.

6 Top with the pickled red onion and serve.

SWAP IT Leave out the bacon to make this dish veggie. Swap out any of the herbs for whatever you have in the fridge – parsley or basil would also work really well here.

**Prep + cook time
15 minutes
Serves 2–3**

SWEETHEART CABBAGE WITH CHILLI GARLIC BUTTER

30g (2 tbsp) unsalted butter, softened
½ red chilli, deseeded and finely chopped
1 clove of garlic, crushed
1 sweetheart cabbage, cut lengthways into quarters
1 tbsp finely chopped chives
1 tbsp crispy chilli oil

1 In a small bowl combine the butter, red chilli, and garlic, mixing well.
2 Add the cabbage to a large microwaveable bowl, then dot over the chilli garlic butter. Cover and cook in the microwave for 6 minutes until the cabbage is tender.
3 Sprinkle over the chives, drizzle over the chilli oil, and serve.

SERVE IT This cabbage makes for a really impressive side dish to go alongside chicken or fish, or you could even serve it as a veggie main for one!

**Prep + cook time
8 minutes
Serves 2**

GREEN BEANS WITH CRISPY SHALLOTS

1 tsp Dijon mustard
1 banana shallot, thinly sliced
2 tbsp sherry vinegar
1 tsp maple syrup
4 tsp extra virgin olive oil
250g (9oz) green beans, trimmed
2 tbsp finely chopped chives
1 quantity Crispy Shallots (see p11)
salt and freshly ground black pepper

1 To a small bowl, add the Dijon mustard, sliced shallot, sherry vinegar, maple syrup, and olive oil. Season with salt and freshly ground black pepper. Whisk well until thickened, then set aside.

2 Add the green beans to a large microwaveable bowl with 2 tablespoons of water. Cover and cook on the higher setting for 3 minutes until tender.

3 To serve, spoon the dressing over the green beans, then sprinkle over the crispy shallots and chopped chives.

SERVE IT These tangy green beans are a tasty companion to a steak or microwaved sweet jacket potato.

Prep + cook time
5 minutes
Serves 2

CAULIFLOWER SALAD WITH TAHINI DRESSING

50g (⅓ cup) walnut halves
1 tbsp vegetable oil
½ red onion, thinly sliced
juice of 1 lemon
½ cauliflower, cut into florets
400g (14oz) can butter beans, drained and rinsed
100g (3½oz) kale, stalks removed and roughly chopped
2 tbsp tahini
1 tsp soy sauce
juice of ½ lime
1 tbsp Greek yogurt
salt and freshly ground black pepper

1 Add the walnuts to a microwaveable plate, drizzle over the vegetable oil, then mix well so the nuts are coated. Lay out flat on the plate and cook, uncovered, in the microwave for 3 minutes until they smell toasty. Roughly chop, then set aside.

2 To a small bowl, add the red onion and lemon juice. Season with a pinch of salt and scrunch together with your hands, then set aside to pickle lightly.

3 Put the cauliflower in a large microwaveable bowl, add 2 tablespoons of water, then cover and cook for 4 minutes.

4 Add the butter beans and kale to the bowl, then season with salt and freshly ground black pepper. Cover and cook for 3 minutes until the cauliflower is tender and the kale has softened.

5 Meanwhile, to a small bowl, add the tahini, soy, lime juice, yogurt, and 100ml (6½ tablespoons) of water. Whisk well until thick, and set aside.

6 Pour the dressing over the salad, top with the pickled red onion, then scatter over the walnuts and serve.

SWAP IT To make this vegan, swap the Greek yogurt for a plant-based alternative.

KEEP IT This is a great salad for meal prepping – store it in the fridge for up to 2 days, keeping the dressing separate.

Prep + cook time
12 minutes
Serves 2

BRAISED RED CABBAGE

1 red cabbage, shredded
1 red onion, thinly sliced
1 tsp caraway seeds
1 tbsp soft dark brown sugar
80ml (⅓ cup) balsamic vinegar
20g (1½ tbsp) unsalted butter
handful of flat-leaf parsley,
    roughly chopped

1 To a large microwaveable bowl, add the cabbage, red onion, caraway seeds, sugar, balsamic vinegar, and 2 tablespoons of water. Cover and cook for 10 minutes.
2 Stir, then cook for a further 5 minutes until the cabbage has completely softened.
3 Add the butter and stir. Top with the parsley and serve.

TIP This can be made a day ahead of time, and simply reheated for 4 minutes before serving. Perfect for Christmas day prep.

**Prep + cook time
15 minutes
Serves 4**

LEMONY BUTTERNUT SQUASH & QUINOA SALAD

½ butternut squash, peeled and cut into 3cm (1¼-inch) chunks
250g (9oz) microwaveable packet of quinoa
2 tbsp pumpkin seeds
large handful of salad leaves
salt and freshly ground black pepper

DRESSING:
100g (3½oz) feta
handful of coriander
handful of flat-leaf parsley
grated zest and juice of 1 lemon
50ml (3½ tbsp) extra virgin olive oil

1 Put the butternut squash and 2 tablespoons of water into a large microwaveable bowl. Cover and cook in the microwave for 8 minutes until the butternut squash is tender. Set aside to cool.
2 Cook the quinoa in the microwave for 2 minutes, or according to the packet instructions, then set aside to cool.
3 Lay the pumpkin seeds out flat on a microwaveable plate, and cook for 2 minutes until the seeds smell lightly toasted.
4 Meanwhile, put all of the dressing ingredients into a blender, and season with salt and freshly ground black pepper. Blitz until smooth, then add a little water if the dressing is looking too thick.

5 Add the salad leaves to a bowl along with the butternut squash and quinoa. Drizzle over the dressing and toss together. Sprinkle over the seeds and serve.

KEEP IT This butternut squash salad is great for prepping ahead – simply keep the salad leaves and dressing separate until ready to assemble. It will also keep for up to 2 days in the fridge.

SWAP IT To make this vegan, simply replace the feta with the same quantity of firm tofu.

Prep + cook time
15 minutes
Serves 2

COURGETTES WITH RED PEPPER DIP

40g (⅓ cup) blanched almonds
2 courgettes, thinly sliced
170g (6oz) jarred roasted red peppers
½ clove of garlic
1 tsp smoked paprika, plus extra
   to serve
1 tbsp sherry vinegar
50ml (3½ tbsp) extra virgin olive oil,
   plus extra to serve
salt and freshly ground black pepper

TO SERVE (OPTIONAL):
crostini or nachos

1 Put the almonds onto a microwaveable plate, then cook, uncovered, in the microwave for 3 minutes until they smell toasted and are golden in colour. Set aside.
2 Put the courgettes into a large microwaveable bowl, and cook for 3 minutes until softened. Set aside.
3 Meanwhile, add three-quarters of the almonds to a blender, then add the jarred peppers, garlic, paprika, sherry vinegar, and olive oil. Season with a little salt and freshly ground black pepper. Pulse until combined, but not totally smooth.
4 Roughly chop the remaining almonds, and set aside.

5 Spread the red pepper dip over a small serving platter, then top with the courgettes. Sprinkle over the chopped almonds, drizzle over a little more olive oil, sprinkle over some extra paprika, and serve with nachos or crostini for dipping.

SERVE IT This is a nice alternative dip at a summer BBQ, served with nachos or Paprika Potato Chips (see p60). Alternatively, this would make a delicious side dish to some white fish.

**Prep + cook time
8 minutes
Serves 3–4**

GARLIC BUTTER PRAWNS

100g (7 tbsp) unsalted butter
½ tsp chilli flakes
2 cloves of garlic, thinly sliced
165g (6oz) raw peeled king prawns
handful of flat-leaf parsley
grated zest of 1 lemon
½ tsp smoked paprika
salt and freshly ground black pepper

TO SERVE (OPTIONAL):
baguette slices

1 Add the butter, chilli flakes, and garlic to a small microwaveable bowl. Cook, uncovered, in the microwave on the lowest setting for 2 minutes until the butter has melted.
2 Add the prawns, cover, then cook on the highest setting for 2 minutes until the prawns are cooked through.
3 Sprinkle over the parsley, lemon zest, and paprika. Season with a little salt and freshly ground black pepper, and serve with the baguette slices for dipping.

SERVE IT This dish is perfect as part of a tapas feast – incredibly simple, yet so impressive!

Prep + cook time
7 minutes
Serves 1–2

PAPRIKA POTATO CHIPS

2 large white potatoes,
   very thinly sliced
4 tsp sunflower or vegetable oil
1 tsp paprika, plus extra to serve
salt

TO SERVE (OPTIONAL):
soured cream
finely chopped chives

1 Lay out a piece of baking parchment on a microwaveable plate.
2 Put some of the sliced potatoes on the baking parchment, making sure that they are not touching (you will need to do this in batches). Brush them with some oil and cook, uncovered, for 2 minutes in the microwave.
3 Carefully turn the potato slices over, and cook for a further minute until golden in colour.
4 Remove the potato chips, then sprinkle over some salt and paprika. Set aside to cool, and repeat with the remaining potato slices.

5 Serve with some soured cream mixed with chopped chives, if you like, and sprinkle over an extra pinch of paprika.

SERVE IT Serve with some dips and crudités on the side, and you've got the perfect buffet!

Prep + cook time
10 minutes
Serves 3–4

CHEESY MASHED POTATOES

500g (1lb 2oz) floury potatoes, peeled and cut into 3cm (1¼-inch) chunks
40g (3 tbsp) unsalted butter, plus extra to serve
75ml (5 tbsp) milk
50g (½ cup) grated cheddar
salt and freshly ground black pepper

TO SERVE (OPTIONAL):
finely chopped chives

1 Put the potatoes and 2 tablespoons of water into a large microwaveable bowl. Cover and cook in the microwave for 12 minutes.
2 Add the butter and milk to the bowl, cover, and cook for 30 seconds more. Remove from the microwave and leave to stand, with the lid on, for 2 minutes.
3 Using a potato masher, mash the potatoes until smooth, then add the cheddar and season with salt and pepper.

4 Top with an extra knob of butter and sprinkle with chopped chives to serve, if liked.

SERVE IT Sausages and gravy are nothing without mash... but by adding cheese, your sausages and mash will be taken to another level!

Prep + cook time
15 minutes
Serves 2

TUNA NICOISE SALAD

¼ red onion, thinly sliced

2 tbsp red wine vinegar

2 tsp maple syrup

200g (7oz) baby new potatoes, halved

100g (3½oz) green beans, trimmed

1 tsp Dijon mustard

40ml (2½ tbsp) extra virgin olive oil

large handful of mixed salad leaves

1 large tomato, roughly chopped

1 tbsp capers

2 tbsp pitted green olives, roughly chopped

145g (5oz) can tuna

handful of dill, roughly chopped

1 tbsp dried oregano

salt and freshly ground black pepper

1 Put the red onion in a small bowl, add 1 tablespoon of red wine vinegar, 1 teaspoon of maple syrup, and a pinch of salt. With your hands, scrunch together, then set aside to pickle lightly.

2 Add the potatoes to a large microwaveable bowl, then cover and cook in the microwave for 6 minutes.

3 Add the green beans, cover, and cook for a further 3 minutes until both the potatoes and green beans are tender. Set aside to cool slightly.

4 Meanwhile, to a small bowl, add the remaining 1 tablespoon of red wine vinegar and 1 teaspoon of maple syrup, along with the Dijon mustard and olive oil. Season with salt and freshly ground black pepper, and whisk until thick but pourable. Set aside.

5 To a large bowl, add the salad leaves, tomato, capers, olives, tuna, green beans, and potatoes. Drizzle over the dressing, and toss everything together. Top with the pickled red onion, dill, and oregano.

KEEP IT You can cook the green beans and potatoes up to 2 days before assembling the salad – just keep them in the fridge until ready to serve.

Prep + cook time
12 minutes
Serves 2

ZINGY AUBERGINES

1 aubergine, cut into
   4cm (1½-inch) chunks
2 tbsp soy sauce
1 tbsp rice wine vinegar
1 tsp mirin
1 tsp crispy chilli oil, plus
   extra to serve
1 tsp sesame oil
juice of 1 lime
handful of coriander, finely chopped
1 red chilli, thinly sliced
2 tbsp roasted peanuts, roughly
   chopped

1 Put the aubergine chunks into a large microwaveable bowl, then add the soy, vinegar, mirin, crispy chilli oil, and sesame oil. Leave to marinate for 20 minutes.
2 Once marinated, cover and cook in the microwave for 12 minutes until the aubergine chunks have completely softened.
3 Squeeze over the lime juice, then top with the coriander, red chilli, peanuts, and extra chilli oil to serve.

SERVE IT These zingy aubergines are so fresh. They would make an impressive side dish to Chicken with Crackling, Rice & Dipping Sauces (see p88).

**Prep + cook time
15 minutes, plus
marinating time
Serves 2**

BRUSSELS SPROUTS WITH PANCETTA & BLUE CHEESE

70g (2½oz) diced pancetta
500g (1lb 2oz) Brussels sprouts,
   trimmed and halved
75g (2½oz) blue cheese
small handful of chives,
   finely chopped

1 Put the pancetta into a large microwaveable bowl, then cook in the microwave, uncovered, for 5 minutes until golden in colour. Remove the pancetta, set aside, and keep the oil in the bowl.
2 Add the Brussels sprouts to the pancetta oil and mix. Cover and cook for 4 minutes until tender.
3 Sprinkle the pancetta over the Brussels sprouts, crumble over the blue cheese, and finish with a scattering of chives.

SWAP IT This dish would still be excellent with just blue cheese, if you want to keep it veggie and omit the pancetta.

**Prep + cook time
10 minutes
Serves 2**

CREAMY SPINACH GRATIN

600g (1lb 5oz) frozen spinach
½ onion, finely chopped
1 clove of garlic, crushed
1 tbsp extra virgin olive oil
100ml (6½ tbsp) double cream
100g (½ cup) cream cheese
grated zest and juice of
   1 lemon
50g (½ cup) grated cheddar
salt and freshly ground
   black pepper

TO SERVE (OPTIONAL):
chopped dill

1 Put the spinach in a small microwaveable dish, then cover and cook in the microwave for 3 minutes until the spinach has defrosted. Remove the spinach from the bowl, then squeeze out as much water as you can. Set aside.

2 Put the onion and garlic into the same bowl and drizzle over the olive oil. Cover and cook in the microwave on the low setting for 2 minutes until the onion has softened.

3 Add the spinach back to the bowl, then add the double cream, cream cheese, lemon zest, lemon juice, and cheddar. Season with salt and pepper and mix well. Cover and cook for 3 minutes.

4 Mix again, and serve with a scattering of dill, if liked.

SERVE IT Take a Sunday roast chicken up a notch by serving it with this delicious side dish. Serve alongside some roast potatoes and gravy, then simply wait for the compliments.

**Prep + cook time
10 minutes
Serves 4**

MAINS

The main event! This chapter will show you just how easy it is to put together delicious, nourishing, and fresh meals, often using just one bowl. All of these dishes are full of flavour, and you won't believe how quickly you can achieve them. You will find something here for every mood, season, and craving.

BUTTERNUT SQUASH RISOTTO

½ butternut squash,
   peeled and cut into
   3cm (1¼-inch) chunks
200g (1 generous cup)
   risotto rice
550ml (2¼ cups) hot
   vegetable stock
70g (1 cup) finely grated
   Parmesan, plus extra
   to serve
15g (1 tbsp) unsalted butter
grated zest and juice of
   1 lemon
small handful of sage leaves
2 tbsp extra virgin olive oil
salt and freshly ground
   black pepper

1 Put the butternut squash into a large microwaveable bowl. Cover and cook in the microwave for 6 minutes until tender.

2 Set one-third of the butternut squash aside, then put the rest into a blender, add a little water, and blitz until smooth.

3 Add the blitzed squash back to the large bowl, then add the risotto rice and stock. Cover and cook for 10 minutes, then stir, and cook for a further 5 minutes until the rice is tender and the stock has been absorbed.

4 Add the Parmesan, butter, and lemon zest and juice. Season well with salt and freshly ground black pepper, and mix well.

5 Fry the sage leaves in the olive oil until crispy, then slice and serve on top, along with the remaining butternut squash chunks and some extra Parmesan.

SWAP IT Crispy sage is the perfect partner to the sweetness of the butternut squash, but if you don't fancy the sage, then a crumbling of some salty blue cheese on top would also work well.

**Prep + cook time
25 minutes
Serves 2–3**

SPAGHETTI VONGOLE

200g (7oz) spaghetti
1 banana shallot, finely chopped
1 large tomato, deseeded and
    finely chopped
1 red chilli, deseeded and
    finely chopped
20g (1½ tbsp) unsalted butter
4 tsp white wine
500g (1lb 2oz) clams,
    scrubbed clean
juice of 1 lemon
handful of flat-leaf parsley,
    finely chopped
salt and freshly ground
    black pepper

TO SERVE (OPTIONAL):
lemon wedges

1 Add the spaghetti to the large microwaveable bowl, you may need to break the spaghetti to fit it in. Add 500ml (2 cups) of water, cover, and cook in the microwave for 14 minutes until most of the water has been absorbed and the pasta is tender, then set aside.

2 To a large microwaveable bowl, add the shallot, tomato, red chilli, butter, white wine, and clams. Cover and cook for 5 minutes until the clams have opened. Discard any clams that have not opened.

3 Tip the spaghetti into the bowl, add the lemon juice, season with salt and freshly ground black pepper, and mix well. Sprinkle over the parsley and serve with lemon wedges, if liked.

SWAP IT You can also use other shellfish, such as mussels or prawns instead of the clams.

**Prep + cook time
20 minutes
Serves 2–3**

HARISSA SALMON

100g (generous ½ cup) couscous
juice of 1 lemon
1 tbsp harissa
1 tsp honey
1 clove of garlic, crushed
2 salmon fillets
handful of mint, roughly chopped
handful of basil, roughly chopped
200g (1½ cups) canned chickpeas
(drained weight), rinsed
1 tbsp capers
½ red onion, finely chopped
salt and freshly ground black pepper

1 Fill a kettle with water and boil. Add the couscous to a medium bowl, then pour over the boiling water until just covered. Add the juice of half of the lemon, cover, and leave to sit for 10 minutes.

2 Meanwhile, to a small bowl, add the juice of the remaining half a lemon, the harissa, honey, and garlic, then set aside.

3 Put the salmon into a large microwaveable bowl or onto a microwaveable plate. Pour the harissa marinade over the salmon, then cover and cook for 2 minutes. Remove from the microwave, leaving it covered for a further 2 minutes until the salmon is cooked through.

4 Meanwhile, fluff up the couscous with a fork, then add the mint, basil, chickpeas, capers, and red onion. Season with salt and freshly ground black pepper, and mix well.

5 Serve the salmon over the couscous.

SWAP IT Swap out the herbs in the couscous for whatever you have in the fridge – coriander or dill would also work well.

Prep + cook time
15 minutes
Serves 2

LOADED SWEET POTATOES

2 sweet potatoes
400g (14oz) can black beans, drained and rinsed
2 tsp chipotle paste
1 tsp maple syrup
1 avocado
1 tbsp soured cream
juice of 1 lime
handful of coriander, roughly chopped
1 green chilli, finely chopped
salt

1 Prick the sweet potatoes several times with a fork. Put onto a microwaveable plate, and cook in the microwave, uncovered, for 5–6 minutes until soft. Remove and set aside.

2 Meanwhile, add the black beans to a small microwaveable bowl, add the chipotle paste, then mix. Cover and cook for 2 minutes until the beans are warm. Add the maple syrup, then set aside.

3 To a small bowl, add the avocado, then mash with a fork. Add the soured cream, lime juice, and coriander. Season with some salt, then mix and set aside.

4 Slice the potatoes in half lengthways, then top with the black beans and avocado. Finish by adding the chopped green chilli.

SWAP IT The toppings on these sweet potatoes are easily adaptable – using crispy bacon and cheese would also work well here.

**Prep + cook time
10 minutes
Serves 2**

AUBERGINE
PARMIGIANA

2 aubergines, cut lengthways into
    2cm (¾-inch) slices
2 tbsp extra virgin olive oil
400g (14oz) can chopped tomatoes
100g (1¼ cups) dried breadcrumbs
handful of basil, leaves picked
20g (⅓ cup) finely grated Parmesan
50g (scant ½ cup) pre-grated
    mozzarella
salt and freshly ground
    black pepper

1 Put the aubergine slices into a large microwaveable bowl, then drizzle over the olive oil and season with salt and freshly ground black pepper. Cover and cook in the microwave for 5 minutes until softened, then remove the aubergine slices from the bowl.

2 To the empty bowl, add enough of the chopped tomatoes to cover the base of the dish, then add some breadcrumbs, basil, and Parmesan. Finally, layer over the aubergines making sure they don't overlap. Repeat this process again until all of those ingredients have been used.

3 Sprinkle over the mozzarella, then cook, uncovered, for 12 minutes until bubbling.

**Prep + cook time
20 minutes
Serves 3–4**

STEAK & KIMCHI WITH DIPPING SAUCE

50g (⅔ cup) mushrooms (shiitake, enoki, or chestnut), thinly sliced

100g (⅔ cup) frozen sweetcorn

250g (9oz) pak choi, cut lengthways into quarters

250g (9oz) sirloin steak, fat removed and very thinly sliced

2 tbsp soy sauce

1 tbsp sesame oil

1 tsp crispy chilli oil

2 tbsp kimchi

1 tbsp sesame seeds

TO SERVE:

250g (9oz) microwaveable packet of sticky rice

DIPPING SAUCE:

2 tbsp soy sauce

1 tbsp rice wine vinegar

1 tsp crispy chilli oil

1 tsp mirin

1 In a large microwaveable bowl, layer the ingredients one on top of the other, starting with the mushrooms, then the sweetcorn, pak choi, and steak slices.

2 Add the soy, sesame oil, and crispy chilli oil, then pour over 100ml (6½ tablespoons) of water.

3 Cover and cook in the microwave for 4 minutes until the vegetables are tender and the steak is cooked through.

4 Meanwhile, to a small bowl, add all the dipping sauce ingredients, whisk, and set aside.

5 Remove the bowl from the microwave, then top with the kimchi and sesame seeds.

6 Microwave the rice according to the packet instructions and serve it on the side.

SWAP IT To make this veggie, replace the steak with cubes of firm tofu.

Prep + cook time
10 minutes
Serves 2

TOMATO CHICKPEA CURRY

2 cloves of garlic, crushed
½ onion, finely chopped
1cm (½-inch) piece of ginger,
   finely chopped
1 tbsp Madras curry powder
¼ tsp ground turmeric
1 tbsp extra virgin olive oil
400g (14oz) can chopped tomatoes
1 large tomato, grated
400g (14oz) can chickpeas,
   drained and rinsed
juice of 1 lime
handful of coriander,
   roughly chopped
salt

TO SERVE (OPTIONAL):
naan
raita

1 In a shallow microwaveable bowl, combine the garlic, onion, ginger, curry powder, turmeric, and olive oil. Cook, uncovered, on a low setting in the microwave for 3 minutes until fragrant.

2 Add both the chopped tomatoes, grated tomato, and the chickpeas, then cover and cook in the microwave on the highest setting for 6 minutes.

3 Add the lime juice, season with salt, and finish by adding the coriander.

4 Serve with naan and some raita, if liked.

**Prep + cook time
10 minutes
Serves 2**

CHICKEN WITH CRACKLING, RICE & DIPPING SAUCES

2 spring onions, sliced,
  plus extra to serve
2cm (¾-inch) piece of ginger,
  finely chopped
2 tbsp vegetable or sunflower oil
1 tbsp sesame oil
1 tsp rice wine vinegar
4 boneless chicken thighs
200g (1 cup plus 2 tbsp)
  basmati rice
large handful of coriander,
  finely chopped
2 tbsp soy sauce
1 tbsp fish sauce
1 tsp crispy chilli oil
1 clove of garlic, crushed
juice of 1 lime
1 tsp caster sugar
salt

1 Add the spring onions, ginger, and vegetable oil to a small microwaveable bowl. Cover and cook on a low setting in the microwave for 2 minutes until fragrant. Add the sesame oil and rice wine vinegar, then set aside.

2 Remove the skin from the chicken thighs, and add the skin to a large microwaveable bowl. Cover and cook on a low setting in the microwave for 12 minutes, checking in 2-minute intervals, until crispy. Remove the chicken skin and set it aside, leaving the chicken fat that is left behind in the bowl.

3 Add the rice to the reserved chicken fat, then add 400ml (1¾ cups) of water and a pinch of salt. Cut the chicken thighs into 2cm (¾-inch) pieces, and add them to the bowl.

4 Cover and cook in the microave on the highest setting for 12 minutes until the water has been absorbed and the rice is tender.

5 Meanwhile, to a small bowl, add the coriander, soy, fish sauce, crispy chilli oil, garlic, lime juice, and sugar. Mix well and set aside.

6 Serve the chicken and rice with the two dipping sauces on the side. Crumble the chicken skin over and serve with extra spring onion slices on top.

TIP The chicken fat is the secret to this delicious rice, and the crackling gives an unbelievable flavour and crunch.

**Prep + cook time
30 minutes
Serves 2**

AUBERGINE DONBURI

2 spring onions, thinly sliced
2cm (¾-inch) piece of ginger,
  finely chopped
3 tbsp vegetable oil
1 tbsp white wine vinegar
1 large aubergine, sliced lengthways
  into 2cm (¾-inch) thick slices
2 tbsp soy sauce
1 tbsp fish sauce
juice of ½ lime
1 tbsp mirin
1 tsp maple syrup
1 clove of garlic, crushed
salt

TO SERVE:
250g (9oz) microwaveable packet
  of basmati rice
1 tbsp Crispy Shallots (see p11)

1 In a small microwaveable bowl, combine the spring onions, ginger, and 2 tablespoons of vegetable oil. Cover and cook on a low setting in the microwave for 2 minutes until the spring onions have softened and are fragrant. Add in the white wine vinegar and a pinch of salt, then set aside.

2 Add the aubergine slices to a large microwaveable bowl, then pour over the remaining tablespoon of oil. Cover and cook in the microwave on the highest setting for 6 minutes.

3 Meanwhile, to a small bowl, add the soy, fish sauce, lime juice, mirin, maple syrup, and garlic, and mix well.

4 Pour the sauce over the aubergine, cover, and cook for 2 minutes.

5 Microwave the rice according to the packet instructions.

6 Serve the aubergine with the rice, and top with the spring onion dressing and crispy shallots.

Prep + cook time
12 minutes
Serves 2

SAUSAGE & CREAMY LEMON BUTTER BEANS

4 sausages

400g (14oz) can butter beans, drained and rinsed

1 banana shallot, finely chopped

1 clove of garlic, crushed

100ml (6½ tbsp) vegetable stock

juice of 1 lemon

50g (1 scant cup) spinach

handful of mint, finely chopped

handful of basil, finely chopped

handful of flat-leaf parsley, finely chopped

2 cornichons, finely chopped

1 tbsp red wine vinegar

½ tsp caster sugar

50ml (3½ tbsp) extra virgin olive oil

1 tbsp crème fraîche

salt and freshly ground black pepper

1 Put the sausages onto a shallow microwaveable plate, then prick the sausage skins with a fork several times. Cover and cook in the microwave for 3 minutes until the sausages are cooked through, then set aside.

2 To a large microwaveable bowl, add the butter beans, shallot, garlic, and vegetable stock. Season with salt and freshly ground black pepper, then cover and cook for 6 minutes. Remove the cover, then cook, uncovered, for 3 minutes.

3 Add the lemon juice, spinach, and sausages. Cover and cook for 2 minutes until the spinach has wilted.

4 Meanwhile, to a small bowl, add the mint, basil, parsley, cornichons, red wine vinegar, sugar, and olive oil. Season with a pinch of salt, and set aside.

5 Remove the bowl from the microwave, then stir through the crème fraîche.

6 Serve topped with the herby dressing.

SWAP IT These beans would also work with other protein foods, such as chicken or salmon. Swap out the sausages for veggie ones, if you prefer.

Prep + cook time
15 minutes
Serves 2

STEAMED SEA BASS WITH POTATOES & GARLIC MAYO

400g (14oz) new potatoes, halved
handful of chives, finely chopped
10g (2 tsp) unsalted butter
2 sea bass fillets
½ orange, thinly sliced
1 lemon, thinly sliced
2 sprigs of rosemary
40g (scant ½ cup) pitted black olives
1 tbsp capers
2 tbsp extra virgin olive oil
salt and freshly ground black pepper

GARLIC MAYO:
1 bulb of Confit Garlic (see p11)
100g (7 tbsp) mayonnaise

1 Put the potatoes in a large microwaveable bowl, add 2 tablespoons of water, cover, then cook in the microwave for 9 minutes until tender. Add the chives and butter, season with salt and freshly ground black pepper, mix, and set aside.

2 Put the sea bass fillets on a large piece of baking parchment. Top the fish with the orange and lemon slices, rosemary, black olives, and capers. Season with salt and freshly ground black pepper, then drizzle over the olive oil. Bring the two long edges of the baking parchment together, then fold over several times to seal like a parcel, doing the same with the two short edges.

3 Put the fish parcel on a microwaveable plate, and cook for 4 minutes until the fish is opaque.

4 For the garlic mayo, squeeze the cooked softened garlic out of its skin into a small bowl. Add the mayonnaise, then mix and set aside.

5 Unwrap the parcel, then serve with the potatoes and garlic mayo on the side.

KEEP IT The fish parcels can be assembled and kept in the fridge until you are ready to cook.

SWAP IT Salmon or cod would also work really well here.

Prep + cook time
15 minutes
Serves 2

COTTAGE PIE

600g (1lb 5oz) floury potatoes,
    peeled and cut in 3cm (1¼-inch)
    chunks
90ml (⅓ cup) milk
60g (½ stick) unsalted butter
1 large carrot, peeled and finely
    chopped
1 stick of celery, finely chopped
1 tbsp extra virgin olive oil
400g (14oz) beef mince
1 tbsp tomato purée
2 tbsp gravy granules
1 tbsp Marmite
a few sprigs of thyme
salt and freshly ground
    black pepper

1 Put the potatoes in a large microwaveable bowl, add 2 tablespoons of water, cover, then cook in the microwave for 12 minutes until the potatoes are soft.
2 Add milk and butter, then cook for a further 30 seconds. Remove from the microwave and let the potatoes sit for 2 minutes. Transfer to another bowl, then mash with a potato masher and set aside.
3 To the microwaveable bowl, add the carrot, celery, and olive oil. Add 2 tablespoons of water, cover, and cook for 8 minutes until the vegetables have softened.
4 Add the beef, tomato purée, gravy granules, Marmite, thyme, and 100 ml (6½ tablespoons) of water. Season with salt and freshly ground black pepper, mix well, then cover and cook for 5 minutes.

5 Discard the thyme, then use a wooden spoon to break up the mince.
6 Top with the mashed potatoes. Cover and cook in the microwave for 4 minutes until bubbling.

TIP You are saving time by cooking this family classic in the microwave. If you wish, you can save even more time by using ready-made mash for the topping.

**Prep + cook time
35 minutes
Serves 3–4**

FISH STEW

3 cloves of garlic, crushed
1 banana shallot, finely chopped
1 tsp fennel seeds
1 tbsp extra virgin olive oil
400g (14oz) can chopped tomatoes
pinch of saffron
250g (9oz) mussels, scrubbed clean
100g (3½oz) piece of cod, cut into
    4cm (1½-inch) chunks
4 large raw peeled king prawns
2 tbsp mayonnaise
1 tsp Dijon mustard
handful of flat-leaf parsley,
    roughly chopped
salt and freshly ground
    black pepper

TO SERVE:
baguette slices
lemon wedges

1 To a large microwaveable bowl, add the garlic, shallot, fennel seeds, and olive oil. Cook in the microwave, uncovered, on the lowest setting for 2 minutes until softened.
2 Add the chopped tomatoes, saffron, and mussels. Season with salt and freshly ground black pepper, then cover and cook on the highest setting for 4 minutes.
3 Add the cod and prawns, then cover and cook for a further 1 minute and 30 seconds until the mussel shells are fully open and the cod and prawns are cooked through. Discard any mussels that have not opened.

4 Meanwhile, in a small bowl, combine the mayonnaise and Dijon mustard, mixing well. Set aside.
5 Sprinkle the chopped parsley over the stew, then serve with the mustard mayo, baguette slices for dipping, and lemon wedges on the side.

TIP This fish stew is seriously impressive! It could be made with only the prawns, or the cod, or the mussels, if preferred – just adjust the timings to suit.

**Prep + cook time
10 minutes
Serves 2**

KALE PESTO PASTA

50g (⅓ cup) walnut halves
1 tbsp vegetable or sunflower oil
100g (3½oz) kale, stalks removed
    and roughly chopped
200g (7oz) dried pasta
large handful of basil
½ clove of garlic, roughly chopped
grated zest of 1 lemon
2 tbsp finely grated Parmesan,
    plus extra to serve
100ml (6½ tbsp) extra virgin
    olive oil
salt and freshly ground
    black pepper

1 Add the walnuts to a microwaveable plate, drizzle over the vegetable oil, and mix well so the nuts are coated. Arrange the walnuts flat on the plate, and cook in the microwave, uncovered, for 3 minutes until they smell toasty. Set aside.

2 To a large microwaveable bowl, add the kale with 2 tablespoons of water. Cover and cook for 3 minutes until softened. Remove the kale from the bowl and set aside.

3 Add the pasta to the large microwaveable bowl. If using spaghetti you may need to break it up to fit it in. Add 500ml (2 cups) of water, then cover and cook for 14 minutes until most of the water has been absorbed and the pasta is tender.

4 Meanwhile, to a blender, add the walnuts, kale, basil, garlic, lemon zest, Parmesan, and olive oil. Season with some salt and freshly ground black pepper, then blitz until combined but still retaining some texture.

5 When the pasta is cooked, add the pesto and mix well. Serve with lots of extra Parmesan to finish.

SWAP IT This pesto is easily adaptable. Instead of walnuts, you could use pistachios or pine nuts. You can also just use basil instead of kale, or vice versa.

KEEP IT The pesto can be made ahead of time and stored in a jar for up to a week.

**Prep + cook time
20 minutes
Serves 2**

LEMONY BORLOTTI BEAN BROTH

2 cloves of garlic, crushed
½ onion, finely chopped
1 tbsp extra virgin olive oil
1 small courgette, roughly chopped
400g (14oz) can borlotti beans,
    drained and rinsed
500ml (2 cups) vegetable stock
100g (2 scant cups) spinach
juice of 2 lemons
handful of dill
handful of chives, finely chopped
salt and freshly ground black pepper

TO SERVE:
grated Parmesan

1 In a large microwaveable bowl, combine the garlic, onion, and olive oil. Cook, uncovered, on a low setting in the microwave for 2 minutes until the onion has softened.
2 Add the courgette, borlotti beans, and vegetable stock to the bowl, then cover and cook in the microwave on the highest setting for 4 minutes until the courgette is tender.
3 Add the spinach, cover, then cook for 1 minute until the spinach has just wilted.
4 Add the lemon juice, and season well with salt and freshly ground black pepper.

5 Divide between two bowls and top with the dill and chives. Grate over some Parmesan to serve.

SWAP IT Adapt the recipe to whatever is in your store cupboard and fridge. Butter beans or chickpeas would also work well here, and you could swap the courgette or spinach for kale.

Prep + cook time
10 minutes
Serves 2

103

LAKSA WITH PRAWNS

100g (3½oz) instant rice noodles
2 tbsp laksa paste
400g (14oz) can coconut milk
2 tbsp soy sauce
1 tbsp fish sauce
300ml (1¼ cups) chicken stock
1 tbsp smooth peanut butter
1 tsp caster sugar
165g (6oz) raw king prawns
100g (1¾ cups) beansprouts
juice of 1 lime

TO SERVE (OPTIONAL):
1 tbsp crispy chilli oil
2 tbsp Crispy Shallots (see p11)
1 red chilli, thinly sliced
handful of coriander,
   roughly chopped

1 Fill a kettle with water and boil. Put the noodles in a large bowl and cover them with the boiling water. Leave to soak for 3 minutes.

2 Meanwhile, to a large microwaveable bowl, add the laksa paste, coconut milk, soy, fish sauce, chicken stock, peanut butter, and caster sugar. Cover and cook in the microwave for 2 minutes.

3 Add the prawns and beansprouts, then cover and cook for a further 2 minutes until the prawns are cooked through. Add the lime juice.

4 Drain the noodles and divide between bowls. Add the laksa, and top with crispy chilli oil, crispy shallots, red chilli, and coriander, if liked.

SWAP IT To make this veggie, swap the prawns for some extra veg, such as pak choi or courgettes, or some tofu puffs, if you can get hold of them.

Prep + cook time
8 minutes
Serves 2

MAPO TOFU

2 cloves of garlic, crushed
2cm (¾-inch) piece of ginger, finely chopped
½ onion, finely chopped
1 tbsp vegetable or sunflower oil
2 tbsp white miso paste
1 tbsp soy sauce
1 tbsp oyster sauce
½ tbsp sesame oil
½ tbsp gochujang
1 tbsp soft light brown sugar
200g (7oz) pork mince
350g (12oz) firm silken tofu, cut into 2cm (¾-inch) cubes

TO SERVE:
2 x 250g (9oz) microwaveable packets of basmati rice
1 spring onion, finely chopped
1 tbsp black sesame seeds
1 lime, cut into wedges

1 To a large microwaveable bowl, add the garlic, ginger, and onion. Drizzle over the oil and cook, uncovered, in the microwave on a low setting for 5 minutes.
2 Meanwhile, in a small bowl, combine the miso paste, soy, oyster sauce, sesame oil, gochujang, and brown sugar. Mix together and set aside.
3 Add the pork mince into the large microwaveable bowl, cover, and cook on the highest setting for 2 minutes. Add the sauce mixture, cover, and cook for 2 minutes.
4 Break up the mince with a wooden spoon, add the tofu, then cover and cook for a further 2 minutes.

5 Microwave the rice according to the packet instructions.
6 Serve the mapo tofu with the rice, topped with chopped spring onion sesame seeds, and with lime wedges on the side.

SWAP IT To make this veggie, use veggie mince instead of pork, and use vegetarian oyster sauce.

Prep + cook time
10 minutes
Serves 2

MEATBALLS WITH SPAGHETTI

½ onion, finely chopped
1 clove of garlic, crushed
1 tbsp extra virgin olive oil
200g (7oz) spaghetti
300g (10½oz) beef mince
1 sprig of rosemary, finely chopped
½ tsp dried oregano
1 tsp Marmite
20g (⅓ cup) finely grated Parmesan, plus extra to serve
400g (14oz) can chopped tomatoes
handful of basil, roughly chopped
salt and freshly ground black pepper

1 Add the onion and garlic to a small microwaveable bowl. Drizzle over the olive oil, and cook on a low setting in the microwave for 3 minutes until the onion has softened. Set aside.

2 To a large microwaveable bowl, add the spaghetti. You may need to break the spaghetti to fit it in. Add 450ml (2 scant cups) of water, then cover and cook in the microwave on the highest setting for 14 minutes until most of the water has been absorbed and the pasta is tender. Set aside.

3 To a medium bowl, add the beef mince, rosemary, oregano, Marmite, Parmesan, and onion and garlic. Season with salt and freshly ground black pepper.

4 Roll the mixture into 30g (1oz) balls and put into a large microwaveable bowl, making sure they are not touching. Add the chopped tomatoes. Cover and cook for 4 minutes until the meatballs are cooked through.

5 Add the pasta to the bowl, toss everything together, then stir in the basil. Serve with extra grated Parmesan.

TIP By adding Marmite to the mince, you get the depth of flavour you might miss from not browning the meat in a frying pan.

**Prep + cook time
30 minutes
Serves 2–3**

LAMB KOFTAS

300g (10½oz) lamb mince
1 tbsp harissa
grated zest of 1 lemon
2 cloves of garlic, crushed
4 sprigs of mint, roughly chopped
120g (generous ½ cup) Greek yogurt
handful of basil, roughly chopped
juice of ½ lemon
2 large wraps
1 Little Gem lettuce, shredded
1 large tomato, cut into chunks
3 tbsp pomegranate seeds
100g (3½oz) feta
salt and freshly ground
    black pepper

1 To a medium bowl, add the lamb mince, harissa, lemon zest, garlic, and half of the mint. Season with salt and freshly ground black pepper. Form the mixture into 6 kofta shapes.

2 Put the koftas into a large microwaveable bowl, or onto a microwaveable plate, making sure they are not touching. Cover and cook in the microwave for 4 minutes until cooked through.

3 Meanwhile, to a small bowl, add the yogurt, remaining mint, basil, and lemon juice. Season with salt and freshly ground black pepper, then mix and set aside.

4 Put the wraps onto a microwaveable plate, and cook, uncovered, for 30 seconds until warmed through.

5 To assemble, spread some yogurt onto each wrap, then add the koftas, lettuce, tomato, and pomegranate seeds, then finally crumble over the feta, and serve.

SWAP IT You could use pork mince instead of lamb here, if you prefer.

Prep + cook time
10 minutes
Serves 2

GINGER CHICKEN CONGEE

300g (10½oz) chicken mince
2 cloves of garlic, crushed
2cm (¾-inch) piece of ginger,
    finely chopped
1 tbsp oyster sauce
2 tbsp soy sauce
4 spring onions, finely chopped
handful of coriander, roughly
    chopped
250g (9oz) microwaveable
    packet of sticky rice
250ml (1 cup) vegetable stock
1 tbsp sesame oil
1 tbsp sesame seeds

1 To a medium bowl, add the chicken mince, garlic, ginger, oyster sauce, soy, half the spring onions, and half the coriander. Mix well, then mould the mixture into 20g (¾oz) meatballs.
2 Put the meatballs into a large microwaveable bowl, or onto a microwaveable plate, making sure they are not touching, then cover and cook for 4 minutes until cooked through. Remove and set aside.
3 Squeeze the packet of rice to loosen, then empty the rice into the large microwaveable bowl. Add the vegetable stock, then cover and cook for 3 minutes.

4 Divide the congee between bowls, top with the chicken meatballs and the remaining spring onions and coriander. Drizzle over the sesame oil and sprinkle with the sesame seeds.

SWAP IT To make this veggie, just leave out the chicken – it will be just as delicious without – and replace the oyster sauce with 1 teaspoon white miso paste.

**Prep + cook time
10 minutes
Serves 2**

HERBY COUSCOUS-STUFFED PEPPERS

50g (generous ¼ cup) couscous
juice of 1 lemon
2 peppers, halved and deseeded
1 tbsp extra virgin olive oil
1 large tomato, finely chopped
handful of mint, roughly chopped
handful of basil, roughly chopped
handful of flat-leaf parsley,
    roughly chopped
handful of dill, roughly chopped,
    plus extra to serve
¼ red onion, finely chopped
2 tbsp pitted green olives, finely
    chopped
20g (¾oz) feta
salt and freshly ground
    black pepper

1 Fill a kettle with water and boil. Put the couscous in a medium bowl, then pour over the boiling water until just covered. Add the lemon juice, cover, and leave to sit for 10 minutes.
2 Meanwhile, put the pepper halves into a large microwaveable bowl cut-side up. Drizzle over the olive oil, cover, then cook in the microwave for 3 minutes until they have softened.
3 Fluff up the couscous with a fork, then add the chopped tomato, mint, basil, parsley, dill, red onion, and olives. Season with salt and freshly ground black pepper, then mix well.

4 Fill each of the pepper halves with the couscous mixture, then cover and cook for 2 minutes.
5 Crumble over the feta and serve with extra dill.

SERVE IT These peppers are so quick and impressive to make, and would look fabulous as part of a Mediterranean feast!

SWAP IT To make these vegan, leave out the feta.

Prep + cook time
15 minutes
Serves 2

MAC 'N' CHEESE

70g (2½oz) pancetta
200g (7oz) macaroni
180g (2 cups) grated cheddar
100ml (6½ tbsp) milk
½ tsp cayenne pepper
handful of chives, finely chopped
salt

1 Put the pancetta in a large microwaveable bowl, then cook, uncovered, in the microwave for 5 minutes until golden in colour. Set the pancetta aside, but keep the pancetta oil in the bowl.
2 Add the macaroni to the bowl along with 400ml (1¾ cups) of water. Stir, then cover and cook for 2 minutes.
3 Stir again, then cover and cook for another 4 minutes.
4 Add the cheese, milk, pancetta, and cayenne pepper, then stir.
5 Cover and cook in 30-second intervals for 1 minute until the cheese has melted and liquid has been absorbed.
6 Sprinkle over the chives and serve.

SWAP IT To make this veggie, just leave out the pancetta.

TIP For a fiery kick, add a splash of hot sauce over the top.

**Prep + cook time
15 minutes
Serves 2**

SAUSAGE & SPINACH GNOCCHI BAKE

1 clove of garlic, crushed
1 banana shallot, finely chopped
1 tbsp extra virgin olive oil
4 sausages
300ml (1¼ cups) passata
350g (12oz) gnocchi
50g (1 scant cup) spinach
juice of ½ lemon
125g (generous ½ cup) ricotta
handful of basil
salt and freshly ground black pepper

1 To a large microwaveable bowl, add the garlic and shallot. Drizzle over the olive oil, then cook, uncovered, on the lowest setting in the microwave for 2 minutes.
2 Squeeze the sausages out of their skins into the microwaveable bowl. Cover and cook in the microwave on the highest setting for 2 minutes.
3 Break the sausages up with a wooden spoon, then add the passata, gnocchi, and 50ml (3½ tablespoons) of water. Season well with salt and freshly ground black pepper, and stir. Cover and cook for 4 minutes.

4 Stir, then mix in the spinach and lemon juice. Cover and cook for a further 2 minutes.
5 Stir through the ricotta and sprinkle over the basil, then serve.

SWAP IT Leave out the ricotta and use vegan sausages to make this dish vegan.

TIP Make sure you add a good grind of black pepper – it gives a wonderful kick!

Prep + cook time
10 minutes
Serves 2–3

CAULIFLOWER STEAKS WITH HERBY SAUCE

½ large cauliflower, cut into
 3cm (1¼-inch) thick steaks
1 tsp Dijon mustard
handful of flat-leaf parsley,
 finely chopped
1 tbsp capers, roughly chopped
½ red onion, finely chopped
juice of ½ lemon
2 tbsp extra virgin olive oil
salt and freshly ground black pepper

TO SERVE:
250g (9oz) microwaveable packet
 of Puy lentils

1 To a large microwaveable bowl, add the cauliflower and 2 tablespoons of water. Cover and cook in the microwave for 8 minutes until tender.
2 Meanwhile, to a small bowl, add the Dijon mustard, parsley, capers, red onion, lemon juice, and olive oil. Season with salt and freshly ground black pepper, mix well, then set aside.
3 Heat the pack of Puy lentils according to the packet instructions, then serve with the cauliflower steaks, and spoon over the herby dressing.

KEEP IT This impressive vegan dish can be prepared well ahead of time. Keep the herby dressing in the fridge until ready to serve, then all you have to do is cook the cauliflower and you are good to go!

Prep + cook time
10 minutes
Serves 2

FISH PIE

600g (1lb 5oz) floury potatoes, peeled and cut into 3cm (1¼-inch) chunks
100ml (6½ tbsp) milk
60g (½ stick) unsalted butter
300g (10½oz) pack fish pie mix (salmon, cod and haddock)
150g (scant ¾ cup) cream cheese
80g (⅔ cup) frozen peas
2 tbsp capers, roughly chopped
grated zest of 1 lemon
handful of flat-leaf parsley, roughly chopped
50g (½ cup) grated cheddar
handful of chives, finely chopped
salt and freshly ground black pepper

TO SERVE (OPTIONAL):
lemon wedges

1 To a large microwaveable bowl, add the potatoes and 2 tablespoons of water. Cover and cook in the microwave for 12 minutes until the potatoes are soft.
2 Add the milk and butter, cover, then cook for a further 30 seconds. Remove from the microwave and let the potatoes sit for 2 minutes. Transfer to another bowl, then mash with a potato masher and set aside.
3 Add the fish pie mix to the large microwaveable bowl, then add the cream cheese, peas, capers, lemon zest, and parsley. Season with salt and freshly ground black pepper, and mix well.

4 Top the fish mix with the mashed potatoes and sprinkle the cheese over. Cover and cook for 7 minutes.
5 Sprinkle over the chives, and serve with lemon wedges, if liked.

TIP This is a contender for the easiest fish pie ever! To make it even easier, try using shop-bought mash for the topping.

Prep + cook time
25 minutes
Serves 2–3

CHICKEN TACOS

4 boneless, skinless chicken thighs
1 tbsp fajita seasoning
2 tbsp extra virgin olive oil
2 avocados
1 tbsp soured cream
juice of 1 lime
1 large tomato, deseeded and
   finely chopped
handful of coriander, roughly
   chopped
50g (3½ tbsp) mayonnaise
1 tsp chipotle paste
6–8 small tortilla wraps
1 Little Gem lettuce, shredded
50g (½ cup) grated cheddar
salt

TO SERVE (OPTIONAL):
Crispy Shallots (see p11)
hot sauce
lime wedges

1 To a large microwaveable bowl, add the chicken thighs, fajita seasoning, and olive oil. Season with salt and freshly ground black pepper, then mix well. Cover and cook in the microwave for 5 minutes until cooked through. Shred the chicken, then set aside.

2 Meanwhile, add the avocado to a small bowl and mash with a fork. Add the soured cream, lime juice, and tomato. Season with salt, mix well, and set aside.

3 To a second small bowl, add the mayo and chipotle paste, mix well, and set aside.

4 Add the tortilla wraps to a microwaveable plate and cook in the microwave, uncovered, for 30 seconds until warmed through.

5 To assemble the tacos, add some of the avocado mix to the wraps, then top with some chicken, chipotle mayo, shredded Little Gem, and cheddar. Serve with crispy shallots, hot sauce and lime wedges, if you like.

SWAP IT Prawns instead of chicken work incredibly well; just reduce the cooking time to 3 minutes.

Prep + cook time
15 minutes
Serves 2–3

PORK & PEANUT NOODLES

2 cloves of garlic, crushed

2cm (¾-inch) piece of ginger, finely chopped

1 tbsp sunflower or vegetable oil

400g (14oz) pork mince

3 tbsp crunchy peanut butter

2 tbsp soy sauce

1 tbsp fish sauce

juice of 1 lime

1 tsp crispy chilli oil, plus extra to serve

1 tsp cornflour mixed with 2 tbsp water

200g (7oz) straight-to-wok medium egg or udon noodles

TO SERVE:

handful of coriander, roughly chopped

2 spring onions, finely chopped

2 tbsp salted peanuts, roughly chopped

1 lime, cut into wedges

1 To a large microwaveable bowl, add the garlic, ginger, and oil. Cook, uncovered, on the lowest setting in the microwave for 1 minute.

2 Add the pork mince, cover, then cook in the microave on the highest setting for 4 minutes.

3 Meanwhile, in a small bowl, combine the peanut butter, soy, fish sauce, lime juice, crispy chilli oil, and cornflour mixture. Whisk well and set aside.

4 Break the mince up with a wooden spoon, then add the sauce, along with the noodles. Cover and cook for 3 minutes until the noodles are tender.

5 Sprinkle over the coriander, spring onions, and peanuts, drizzle over a little extra crispy chilli oil, and serve with lime wedges on the side.

**Prep + cook time
10 minutes
Serves 3–4**

SWEET & SOUR CHICKEN

2 chicken breasts, cut into
    4cm (1½-inch) chunks
1 red pepper, cut into
    3cm (1¼-inch) chunks
1 yellow pepper, cut into
    3cm (1¼-inch) chunks
1 onion, thinly sliced
1 tbsp vegetable or sunflower oil
3 tbsp ketchup
1 tsp cornflour mixed with
    1 tbsp water
1 clove of garlic, crushed
2cm (¾-inch) piece of ginger,
    finely chopped
2 tbsp malt vinegar
1 tbsp soy sauce
1 tbsp caster sugar
2 tbsp pineapple juice
80g (3oz) pineapple, peeled, cored
    and cut into 3cm (1¼-inch) chunks

TO SERVE:
250g (9oz) microwaveable
    packet of basmati rice
handful of coriander, roughly
    chopped
2 spring onions, finely chopped

1 To a large microwaveable bowl, add the chicken, both peppers, onion, and oil. Cover and cook in the microwave for 4 minutes.

2 Meanwhile, to a small bowl, add the ketchup, cornflour mixture, garlic, ginger, vinegar, soy, sugar, pineapple juice, and chunks of pineapple. Mix well, then add to the bowl and cook uncovered for 3 minutes.

3 Microwave the rice according to the packet instructions, then serve the sweet and sour chicken with the rice, and sprinkle over the coriander and spring onions.

SWAP IT You could also make this with prawns or firm tofu – just add them in with the sauce for 3 minutes.

**Prep + cook time
10 minutes
Serves 2**

THAI GREEN CHICKEN CURRY

2 tbsp Thai green curry paste
1 tbsp coconut or vegetable oil
2 chicken breasts, cut into
    4cm (1½-inch) chunks
1 aubergine, cut into
    3cm (1¼-inch) chunks
100g (3½oz) Tenderstem broccoli,
    halved horizontally
400g (14oz) can of coconut milk
1 lemongrass stalk, bashed
1 tbsp soy sauce
1 tbsp fish sauce
1 tbsp sugar
juice of 2 limes

TO SERVE:
250g (9oz) microwaveable packet
    of basmati rice

1 Put the curry paste and coconut oil in a large microwaveable bowl, then cook in the microwave, uncovered, on the lowest setting for 1 minute until melted.

2 Add the chicken, aubergine, broccoli, coconut milk, lemongrass, soy, fish sauce, and sugar. Cover and cook in tje microwave on the highest setting for 10 minutes until the chicken is cooked through and the vegetables are tender. Stir through the lime juice.

3 Microwave the rice according to the packet instructions, then serve the curry with the rice.

SWAP IT To make this vegetarian, replace the chicken with some extra veggies, such as courgette or green beans, and use a vegetarian or vegan fish sauce.

**Prep + cook time
15 minutes
Serves 2–3**

SWEET POTATO DAHL

1 clove of garlic, crushed
1 red onion, finely chopped
2cm (¾-inch) piece of ginger,
   finely chopped
1 tbsp sunflower or vegetable oil
200g (7oz) sweet potato, peeled and
   cut into 3cm (1¼-inch) chunks
200g (1 cup plus 2 tbsp) red
   split lentils, rinsed
2 tbsp curry paste
550ml (2¼ cups) vegetable stock
juice of 2 limes
handful of coriander, roughly
   chopped, plus extra to garnish
salt

TO SERVE (OPTIONAL):
Greek yogurt
chapattis or naan breads
Crispy Shallots (see p11)

1 To a large microwaveable bowl, add the garlic, red onion, and ginger. Drizzle over the oil, then cook in the microwave on the lowest setting for 3 minutes until softened.
2 Add the sweet potato, lentils, curry paste, and vegetable stock. Mix well, cover, and cook in the microwave on the highest setting for 7 minutes.
3 Stir, then cook for a further 8 minutes until the lentils and sweet potato are soft, and the water has been absorbed.

4 Stir through the lime juice and coriander.
5 Serve with yogurt, bread, and crispy shallots, if you like, and garnish with extra coriander.

TIP Buy pre-cut sweet potatoes to make this dish even easier to rustle up!

SWAP IT To make this vegan, be sure to use a suitable curry paste and serve with plant-based yogurt.

Prep + cook time
20 minutes
Serves 2

FRENCH ONION SOUP

3 large onions, thinly sliced
2 sprigs of thyme, leaves picked
1 tsp baking powder
500ml (2 cups) beef stock
1 tsp cornflour
1 tbsp Worcestershire sauce
4 baguette slices
50g (scant ½ cup) finely
   grated Gruyere
salt and freshly ground
   black pepper

1 To a large microwaveable bowl, add the sliced onions, thyme, and baking powder. Scrunch together with your hands, then cook in the microwave, uncovered, for 20 minutes, stirring occasionally, until the onions are golden.
2 Add the beef stock, cornflour, and Worcestershire sauce. Season with salt and freshly ground black pepper, then cover and cook for a further 4 minutes.

3 Top with the baguette slices and cheese, then cook, uncovered, for 3 minutes until the cheese has melted.

**Prep + cook time
30 minutes
Serves 2**

CHEESY POLENTA WITH
MUSHROOMS

30g (1 cup) dried porcini mushrooms
200g (2⅔ cups) mushrooms
   (shiitake, oyster, or chestnut),
   thinly sliced
1 tbsp extra virgin olive oil
2 tbsp miso paste
2 tbsp soy sauce
1 tbsp maple syrup
pinch of chilli flakes
90g (⅔ cup) polenta
500ml (2 cups) vegetable stock
100ml (6½ tbsp) milk
30g (2 tbsp) butter
15g (¼ cup) finely
   grated Parmesan
handful of flat-leaf parsley,
   roughly chopped
salt and freshly ground
   black pepper

1 Fill a kettle with water and boil. Add the dried porcini mushrooms to a measuring jug, then pour over the boiling water. Leave to soak for 10 minutes, then roughly chop the mushrooms, and reserve 80ml (⅓ cup) of the soaking liquid. Set both aside.

2 To a large microwaveable bowl, add the fresh mushrooms and olive oil. Season with salt and freshly ground black pepper, then cover and cook in the microwave for 4 minutes.

3 To a small bowl, add the miso paste, soy, maple syrup, chilli flakes, and 2 tablespoons of water, and mix well. Add the sauce to the mushrooms, along with the soaked porcini mushrooms and the reserved porcini liquid. Cook, uncovered, for 3 minutes, then set aside.

4 To a large microwaveable bowl, add the polenta, vegetable stock, and milk. Cover and cook for 7 minutes until most of the liquid has been absorbed. Add the butter, then season generously with salt and freshly ground black pepper, and whisk well until smooth.

5 Divide the polenta between serving plates, top with the mushrooms, then sprinkle over the Parmesan and parsley.

SWAP IT To make this vegan, leave out the Parmesan, replace the butter for plant-based spread and use a vegan alternative milk.

**Prep + cook time
25 minutes
Serves 2–3**

DESSERTS

With the help of the microwave, there are no excuses to avoid whipping up something sweet; no preheating of ovens to make cakes, or standing over the hob nursing a caramel. Create light and fluffy steamed puddings or aromatic fruity crumbles in mere minutes. Sweet treats are no longer reserved for special occasions!

BROWNIES

200g (1 cup) caster sugar

200g (1¾ sticks) unsalted butter, softened

2 eggs

90g (1 scant cup) cocoa powder

70g (½ cup) plain flour

50ml (3½ tbsp) milk

25g (3 tbsp) hazelnuts, roughly chopped

20g (2 tbsp) dark chocolate chips

EQUIPMENT

18cm (7-inch) square microwaveable dish, lightly oiled

1 To a large bowl, add the sugar and butter, then whisk well. Add the eggs, cocoa powder, flour, and milk. Whisk again until smooth.

2 With a spatula, fold in the hazelnuts and chocolate chips. Pour the mix into the oiled microwaveable dish, then cook in the microwave, uncovered, for 5 minutes until firm to the touch.

3 Leave to cool, then slice up and serve.

SWAP IT Try switching the nuts for whatever you have – walnuts, macadamias, or pecans work well.

Prep + cook time
10 minutes
Serves 4–6

POPCORN WITH SALTED CARAMEL SAUCE

60g (2oz) bag of microwaveable popcorn
100g (½ cup) soft light brown sugar
50g (3½ tbsp) salted butter
90ml (6 tbsp) double cream
pinch of sea salt flakes

1 Microwave the popcorn according to the packet instructions, then set aside in a large bowl.
2 To a large microwaveable bowl, add the sugar, butter, and cream. Cook in the microwave, uncovered, in 30-second intervals for 2 minutes until the sugar has dissolved and is syrupy. Be careful when removing it from the microwave, as it will be very hot.
3 Add a pinch of sea salt flakes, then mix well and set aside for a few minutes until safely cooled.

4 Pour the caramel over the popcorn and serve.

TIP Be very careful removing the caramel from the microwave because it will be extremely hot.

Prep + cook time
6 minutes
Serves 4

STICKY RICE WITH MANGO

250g (9oz) microwaveable packet of sticky rice
180ml (¾ cup) coconut milk
2 tbsp caster sugar
1 vanilla pod, cut in half lengthways
1 ripe mango, peeled, stoned, and sliced
grated zest of 1 lime

1 Squeeze the packet to loosen the rice, then put the rice into a small microwaveable bowl.
2 Add the coconut milk, caster sugar, and vanilla pod, then cover and cook for 2 minutes.
3 Stir well, then cover and cook for 2 minutes more until the rice has absorbed the liquid.
4 Divide the rice between bowls and top with the mango and lime zest.

TIP Be sure to use a ripe mango – pre-cut mango chunks would also work well.

Prep + cook time
5 minutes
Serves 2

STEAMED GINGER PUDDING

2 tbsp stem ginger, finely chopped, plus 40ml (2½ tbsp) of the ginger syrup
35g (3 tbsp) caster sugar
35ml (2¼ tbsp) vegetable or sunflower oil
60ml (4 tbsp) milk
75g (½ cup plus 1 tbsp) self-raising flour
½ tsp baking powder
1 tsp white wine vinegar

EQUIPMENT
2 x 200ml (7fl oz) microwaveable moulds, lightly greased

1 Divide the stem ginger syrup between the two greased moulds, and set aside.

2 In a medium bowl, combine half of the stem ginger with the caster sugar, vegetable oil, milk, flour, baking powder, and vinegar. Mix well, then divide between the moulds. Cover with cling film, and cook in the microwave, one at a time, for 1 minute and 30 seconds each.

3 Leave to stand for 4 minutes before turning out onto a plate.

4 Top with the remaining ginger and serve.

TIP To make this even more simple, replace the quantity of stem ginger and ginger syrup with golden syrup.

**Prep + cook time
10 minutes
Serves 2**

CARAMEL BANANAS WITH ICE CREAM

100g (½ cup) soft light
   brown sugar
50g (3½ tbsp) salted butter
90ml (6 tbsp) double cream
2 bananas, peeled and halved
   lengthways

TO SERVE (OPTIONAL):
vanilla ice cream

1 Add the sugar, butter, and cream to a large microwaveable bowl. Cook in the microwave, uncovered, in 30-second intervals for 2 minutes until the sugar has dissolved and the mixture is syrupy.

2 The bowl will be very hot, so add the bananas in very carefully. Cook, uncovered, for 30 seconds until warmed through. Remove from the microwave and leave to cool for a few minutes.

3 Serve the caramel bananas with ice cream on the side, if you like.

SERVE IT These caramel bananas are so addictive and the perfect sweet treat. Ice cream on the side is optional but highly recommended!

**Prep + cook time
5 minutes
Serves 2**

ORANGE DRIZZLE CAKE

2 tbsp honey
grated zest and juice of ½ orange
125g (⅔ cup) caster sugar
125g (9 tbsp) unsalted butter, softened
2 eggs
125g (1 scant cup) self-raising flour
75g (½ cup) icing sugar
1 tbsp milk

TO SERVE (OPTIONAL):
1 orange, thinly sliced
1 tbsp caster sugar

EQUIPMENT

15 x 20cm (6 x 8-inch) shallow microwaveable dish or silicone mould, oiled

1 To a small bowl, add the honey and orange juice, mix well, then set aside.
2 To a medium bowl, add the sugar and butter, then whisk together with electric beaters until pale. Add the eggs, one at a time, whisking between each addition.
3 Add the orange zest and flour, and fold in using a spatula until smooth.
4 Pour the cake batter into the silicone mould, then cover and cook in the microwave for 3 minutes until a skewer comes out clean when inserted.
5 Poke holes in the top of the cake with a skewer, then pour the orange and honey syrup over. Leave to cool for 10 minutes, then remove from the silicone mould and set aside to cool completely.
6 To prepare the oranges, if using, to serve, add the orange slices and sugar to a small microwaveable bowl with 1 tablespoon of water. Cover and cook for 3 minutes until the oranges have softened. Set aside.
7 Meanwhile, to a small bowl add the icing sugar and milk, then whisk well until smooth.
8 Once the cake has cooled, drizzle the icing over and then top with the orange slices, if using. Let set before serving.

SWAP IT You can replace the orange juice with lemon to turn it into a lemon drizzle!

Prep + cook time
20 minutes
Serves 2

CROISSANT CUSTARD BAKE

4 croissants
50g (3 tbsp) raspberry jam
100g (¾ cup) raspberries
250g (9oz) custard
2 tbsp flaked almonds, toasted
(see p11)

EQUIPMENT
19cm (7½-inch) round
microwaveable dish

1 Cut the croissants in half, and spread the raspberry jam on the cut sides.
2 In a large microwaveable dish, arrange the croissants in a single layer, dot the raspberries around them, and pour over the custard.
3 Cook in the microwave, uncovered, for 3 minutes until it is warmed through and the raspberries have turned jammy.

4 Sprinkle the almonds over and serve.

TIP Breakfast or dessert? You decide! The croissants become spongy and soak up the custard, while the raspberries add a tang that cuts through the sweetness.

**Prep + cook time
6 minutes
Serves 4**

STICKY FIG PUDDING

225g (1 cup plus 2 tbsp) soft dark brown sugar
135g (9½ tbsp) unsalted butter, softened
1 egg
75g (½ cup plus 1 tbsp) self-raising flour
80g (½ cup) dried figs, finely chopped
150g (¾ cup) soft light brown sugar
2 tbsp crème fraîche

EQUIPMENT
2 x 200ml (7fl oz) microwaveable moulds, lightly greased and floured

1 To a medium bowl, add 75g (6 tablespoons) of the soft dark brown sugar and 35g (2½ tbsp) of the butter, then cream together using a wooden spoon. Once combined, beat in the egg until smooth.
2 Add the flour and figs, then fold until smooth.
3 Divide the mix between the greased and floured moulds, cover with cling film, and cook in the microwave, one at a time, for 1 minute and 30 seconds each. Leave to cool for 2 minutes, before turning out onto a plate.
4 Meanwhile, to a small microwaveable bowl, add the remaining 150g (¾ cup) of sugar and 100g (7 tbsp) of butter.

5 Cook, uncovered, in 30-second intervals for 2 minutes until the sugar has dissolved and it looks syrupy. Be careful when removing from the microwave as it will be very hot. Stir through the crème fraîche, pour over the puddings, and serve.

SWAP IT Feel free to swap out the figs for dates.

**Prep + cook time
10 minutes
Serves 2**

SPICED APPLE & BLUEBERRY CRUMBLE

500g (1lb 2oz) Bramley apples,
    peeled, cored, and cut into
    3cm (1¼-inch) chunks
200g (1⅔ cups) blueberries
½ tsp ground cardamom
80g (6½ tbsp) soft light brown sugar
juice of ½ lemon
1 tbsp cornflour mixed with
    2 tbsp water
80g (¾ stick) unsalted butter,
    cut into cubes
100g (¾ cup) jumbo oats
50g (scant ½ cup) granola
50g (⅓ cup) plain flour
50g (¼ cup) demerara sugar

EQUIPMENT
15 x 20cm (6 x 8-inch) shallow
    microwaveable dish or silicone
    mould, oiled

1 To the microwaveable dish, add the apples, blueberries, cardamom, soft light brown sugar, lemon juice, and cornflour mixture. Mix well, then cover and cook in the microwave for 4 minutes until the apples are tender and the blueberries have softened. Set aside.

2 Meanwhile, to a medium bowl, add the butter, oats, granola, flour, and demerara sugar. Rub together with your hands until the mixture resembles breadcrumbs.

3 Spoon the crumble topping onto the apples and blueberries, then cook, uncovered, for 4 minutes until the topping is cooked through and hot.

SWAP IT This crumble is easily adaptable. Blackberries or pears would also work well.

Prep + cook time
10 minutes
Serves 4

CARROT CAKE CUPCAKES

60g (½ stick) unsalted butter,
  softened
60g (5 tbsp) caster sugar
2 large (US extra large) eggs
150g (1 generous cup) plain flour
1 tsp baking powder
100g (3½oz) carrots, grated

FROSTING (OPTIONAL):
150g (1¼ sticks) unsalted butter,
  softened
2 tbsp cream cheese
2 tbsp icing sugar

EQUIPMENT
4 x 8cm (3¼-inch) silicone muffin
  cases, lightly oiled
piping bag with a small star nozzle

1 To a medium bowl, add the butter and sugar, then whisk together with electric beaters until pale. Add the eggs, one at a time, whisking between each addition.
2 Add the flour and baking powder, and fold in using a spatula.
3 Fold in the carrots, then divide the mixture among the oiled muffin cases.
4 Cook in the microwave, two at a time, uncovered, for 2 minutes until a skewer comes out clean when inserted.
5 If making the frosting, to a medium bowl, add the butter, cream cheese, and icing sugar. Using electric beaters, whisk on a medium speed until firm.
6 Pipe the buttercream frosting over the cupcakes.

**Prep + cook time
10 minutes
Makes 4**

POMEGRANATE POACHED PEARS

2 pears, peeled and cut in
　　half lengthways
200ml (1 scant cup)
　　pomegranate juice
1 cinnamon stick
4 cloves
50ml (3½ tbsp) maple syrup

TO SERVE (OPTIONAL):
crème fraîche
grated zest of 1 orange

1 In a large microwaveable bowl, arrange the pears in a single layer, cut-side up. Add the pomegranate juice, cinnamon stick, and cloves. Drizzle the maple syrup over the pears, then cover and cook in the microwave for 7 minutes until the pears are tender.

2 Serve with crème fraîche on the side and grated orange zest sprinkled on top, if you like.

TIP The tanginess of the pomegranate juice complements the sweet pears so well. This is a really lovely way to finish a meal.

**Prep + cook time
10 minutes
Serves 2**

COCONUT & LIME CAKE

125g (⅔ cup) caster sugar
125g (9 tbsp) unsalted butter, softened
2 eggs
125g (1 scant cup) plain flour
1 tsp baking powder
70g (1 scant cup) desiccated coconut
grated zest of 2 limes, plus extra to decorate
¼ tsp salt
2 tbsp toasted coconut chips

FROSTING:
80g (¾ stick) unsalted butter, softened
80g (½ cup plus 1 tbsp) icing sugar
1 tsp vanilla extract
180g (generous ¾ cup) cream cheese

EQUIPMENT
20cm (8-inch) round microwaveable dish or silicone mould, oiled

1 To a medium bowl, add the sugar and butter, then whisk together with electric beaters until pale. Add the eggs, one at a time, whisking together between each addition.
2 Fold in the flour, baking powder, desiccated coconut, lime zest, and salt until smooth.
3 Pour the cake batter into the oiled dish, then cover and cook in the microwave for 3 minutes until a skewer comes out clean when inserted.
4 Leave to cool for 10 minutes before removing from the dish, then set aside to cool completely.

5 Meanwhile, for the frosting, to a large bowl add the butter, icing sugar, and vanilla extract. Whisk together with electric beaters until smooth. Add the cream cheese and fold together with a spatula until smooth.
6 Top the cooled cake with the cream cheese frosting, and sprinkle over the coconut chips and extra lime zest to finish.

TIP This is the perfect cake to accompany an afternoon cup of tea.

**Prep + cook time
18 minutes
Serves 4–6**

CHOCOLATE CHIP COOKIE

40g (3 tbsp) unsalted butter
45g (scant ¼ cup) soft light brown sugar
70g (½ cup) plain flour
20g (2 tbsp) dark chocolate chips

1 Add the butter to a small microwaveable bowl, then heat in the microwave, uncovered, in 30-second intervals, for 1 minute until melted.

2 Stir in the soft light brown sugar, flour, and chocolate chips.

3 Shape the cookie mixture into a ball, then put onto a microwaveable plate, and cook in the microwave, uncovered, for 1 minute and 30 seconds until it is fully spread out.

4 Be careful when removing the cookie from the microwave, as it will be very hot. Leave to cool completely before serving.

TIP This recipe is for a single-serve cookie. To make three cookies, triple the ingredient quantities. At the start of step 3, divide the mixture into three portions and cook each cookie one after the other.

**Prep + cook time
5 minutes
Makes 1**

CHOCOLATE MOUSSE WITH WHIPPED CREAM

150g (5¼oz) dark chocolate (70%), roughly chopped
5 eggs, yolks and whites separated
1 tbsp caster sugar
100ml (6½ tbsp) double cream

1 To a large microwaveable bowl, add the chocolate, then heat in the microwave, uncovered, in 30 second intervals for 1 minute and 30 seconds until melted. Set aside.
2 To a large bowl, add the egg whites and sugar. Whisk with electric beaters until you have soft peaks.
3 Add the egg yolks to the melted chocolate and stir through until smooth.
4 Add a large spoonful of the egg whites and fold in with a spatula. Add the remaining egg whites and fold in carefully until fully incorporated.

5 Spoon into 4 glasses or ramekins, and leave to set in the fridge for 2–3 hours.
6 Meanwhile, add the double cream to a medium bowl and whip until you have soft peaks.
7 Once the mousse has set, top each portion with a spoonful of the cream.

TIP This mousse needs enough time to chill in the fridge and set.

**Prep + cook time
15 minutes, plus
chilling time
Serves 4**

ROASTED PLUMS WITH GINGER & WHIPPED CREAM

6 plums, halved and stoned
20g (5 tsp) soft dark brown sugar
30ml (2 tbsp) amaretto or brandy
2cm (¾-inch) piece of ginger,
   finely chopped
grated zest of 1 lime, plus extra
   to decorate
100ml (6½ tbsp) double cream

TO SERVE:
amaretti biscuits, crushed

1 In a large microwaveable bowl, arrange the plums in a single layer, cut-side up. Add the sugar, amaretto, ginger, and lime zest. Cover and cook in the microwave for 4 minutes until the plums are soft.
2 Meanwhile, to a medium bowl, add the cream and whip until thick.
3 Serve the whipped cream alongside the plums, top with the crushed amaretti biscuits and decorate with extra lime zest.

SWAP IT The alcohol can be replaced with fruit juice, such as pomegranate or cranberry.

Prep + cook time
5 minutes
Serves 4–6

CONVERSION CHARTS

MEASURES

North America, New Zealand and the United Kingdom use a 5ml teaspoon and a 15ml tablespoon. North American measuring cups hold approximately 240ml. An Australian metric measuring cup holds approximately 250ml; one Australian metric tablespoon holds 20ml; one Australian metric teaspoon holds 5ml.

The difference between one country's measuring cups and another's is within a two- or three-teaspoon variance and will not affect your cooking results. All cup and spoon measurements are level.

The most accurate way of measuring dry ingredients is to weigh them.

When measuring liquids, use a clear glass or plastic jug with metric markings. We use extra-large eggs with an average weight of 60g each.

DRY MEASURES

metric	imperial
15g	½oz
30g	1oz
60g	2oz
90g	3oz
125g	4oz (¼lb)
155g	5oz
185g	6oz
220g	7oz
250g	8oz (½lb)
280g	9oz
315g	10oz
345g	11oz
375g	12oz (¾lb)
410g	13oz
440g	14oz
470g	15oz
500g	16oz (1lb)
750g	24oz (1½lb)
1kg	32oz (2lb)

LIQUID MEASURES

metric	imperial
30ml	1 fluid oz
60ml	2 fluid oz
100ml	3 fluid oz
125ml	4 fluid oz
150ml	5 fluid oz
190ml	6 fluid oz
250ml	8 fluid oz
300ml	10 fluid oz
500ml	16 fluid oz
600ml	20 fluid oz
1000ml (1 litre)	1¾ pints

LENGTH MEASURES

metric	imperial
3mm	⅛in
6mm	¼in
1cm	½in
2cm	¾in
2.5cm	1in
5cm	2in
6cm	2½in
8cm	3in
10cm	4in
13cm	5in
15cm	6in
18cm	7in
20cm	8in
22cm	9in
25cm	10in
28cm	11in
30cm	12in (1ft)

INDEX

Note: page numbers in **bold** refer
to images.

DK LONDON
Editorial Director Cara Armstrong
Senior Editor Lucy Sienkowska
Senior Designer Tania Gomes
Senior Production Editor Tony Phipps
Senior Production Controller Stephanie McConnell
Design Assistant Izzy Poulson
DTP and Design Coordinator Heather Blagden
Sales Material and Jackets Coordinator Emily Cannings
Publishing Director Stephanie Jackson
Art Director Maxine Pedliham

Author Susanna Unsworth
Editorial Kate Reeves-Brown
Recipe Development and Food Styling Susanna Unsworth
Photography Anthony Duncan
Prop Styling Charlie Phillips

DK DELHI
DTP Designer Satish Gaur
DTP Coordinator Pushpak Tyagi
Pre-production Manager Balwant Singh
Managing Art Editor Neha Ahuja
Creative Head Malavika Talukder

First published in Great Britain in 2025 by
Dorling Kindersley Limited
20 Vauxhall Bridge Road,
London SW1V 2SA

The authorised representative in the EEA is
Dorling Kindersley Verlag GmbH. Arnulfstr. 124,
80636 Munich, Germany

A CIP catalogue record for this book
is available from the British Library.
ISBN: 978-0-2417-4237-2

Printed and bound in China

www.dk.com

ABOUT THE AUTHOR

Susanna Unsworth is a food stylist
and recipe developer based in London.
She trained at Leiths School of Food
and Wine, and has worked as a chef
in restaurants and private kitchens,
and as a food stylist for cookery
books and magazines.

PUBLISHER'S ACKNOWLEDGMENTS

DK would like to thank Rudy Hemming,
Lucy Cottle and Susannah Cohen for
their assistance with food styling,
Nicola Graimes for proofreading and
Lisa Foottit for providing the index.

MIX
Paper | Supporting
responsible forestry
FSC™ C018179

This book was made with Forest
Stewardship Council™ certified
paper – one small step in DK's
commitment to a sustainable future.
**Learn more at www.dk.com/uk/
information/sustainability**